digging

smiling

hugging

sweeping

bouncing

stamping

reading

crawling

sucking

For Jack

First published 1993 by Walker Books Ltd
87 Vauxhall Walk, London SE11 5HJ

This edition published 1995

4 6 8 10 9 7 5 3

This book has been typeset in Plantin.

Printed in Hong Kong

British Library Cataloguing in Publication Data
A catalogue record for this book is
available from the British Library.

ISBN 0-7445-3652-9

Bouncing

Shirley Hughes

WALKER BOOKS
AND SUBSIDIARIES
LONDON • BOSTON • SYDNEY

When I throw my big shiny ball...

it bounces away from me.

Bounce, bounce, bounce, bounce!

Then it rolls along the ground, then it stops.

I like bouncing too. In the mornings
I bounce on my bed,

and the baby bounces in his cot.

Mum and Dad's big bed is an even better
place to bounce.

But Dad doesn't much like being bounced
on in the early morning.

So we roll on the floor instead, and the baby bounces on ME!

After breakfast he
does some dancing
in his baby-bouncer,

and I do some dancing
to the radio.

At my play-group there are big cushions on
the floor where lots of children
can bounce together.

And at home there's a big sofa where we
can bounce when Mum isn't looking.

Grandpa and I know a good bouncing game.

I ride on his knees and we sing:

This is the way the ladies ride: trit-trot, trit-trot;

This is the way the gentlemen ride: tarran, tarran;

This is the way the farmers ride: clip-clop, clip-clop;

This is the way the jockeys ride: gallopy, gallopy,

and FALL OFF!

I like bouncing.

I bounce about all day...

bounce, bounce,
bounce, bounce!

Until in the end I stop
bouncing,

and go off to sleep.

running

painting

looking

drinking

bouncing

counting

sitting

bending

scowling

digging

smiling

hugging

sweeping

bouncing

stamping

reading

crawling

sucking

MORE WALKER PAPERBACKS
For You to Enjoy

Also by Shirley Hughes

BOUNCING / CHATTING / GIVING / HIDING

Each of the books in this series for pre-school children takes a single everyday
verb and entertainingly shows some of its many meanings and applications.

"There's so much to look at, so much to read in
Shirley Hughes' books." *Children's Books of the Year*

0-7445-3652-9	*Bouncing*
0-7445-3654-5	*Chatting*
0-7445-3653-7	*Giving*
0-7445-3655-3	*Hiding*

£4.50 each

OUT AND ABOUT

Eighteen richly-illustrated poems portray the weather and
activities associated with the various seasons.

"Hughes at her best. Simple, evocative rhymes conjure up images that
then explode in the magnificent richness of her paintings." *The Guardian*

0-7445-1422-3   £4.99

TALES FROM TROTTER STREET

"Shirley Hughes is one of the all-time greats and her new series
accurately describes the life of contemporary city kids." *Susan Hill, Today*

0-7445-2032-0	*Angel Mae*	£4.99
0-7445-2033-9	*The Big Concrete Lorry*	£3.99
0-7445-2012-6	*Wheels*	£4.99
0-7445-2357-5	*The Snow Lady*	£4.99

Walker Paperbacks are available from most booksellers, or by post from B.B.C.S., P.O. Box 941, Hull, North Humberside HU1 3YQ
24 hour telephone credit card line 01482 224626

To order, send: Title, author, ISBN number and price for each book ordered, your full name and address,
cheque or postal order payable to BBCS for the total amount and allow the following for postage and packing:
UK and BFPO: £1.00 for the first book, and 50p for each additional book to a maximum of £3.50.
Overseas and Eire: £2.00 for the first book, £1.00 for the second and 50p for each additional book.
Prices and availability are subject to change without notice.